By Tobispartan (Leonardo Gudiño)

ZONE BLACK
Drawing Manual

Line
Dynamic

I0505480

The Dynamic line, like its name
indicates it, makes our work
they look more dynamic; or what is
the same, with movements.

In this guide, you will find a class
many times seen but not taken
in consideration as specified.

The reason is that it became important
keep this class in mind
for this topic so we can help you
more in the handling and movement of
your characters huh even in some
scenarios.

The dynamic line you must apply
in everything so that your works have
higher quality. Keep looking for
other manuals for you to complement
your knowledge and apply it
adequately.

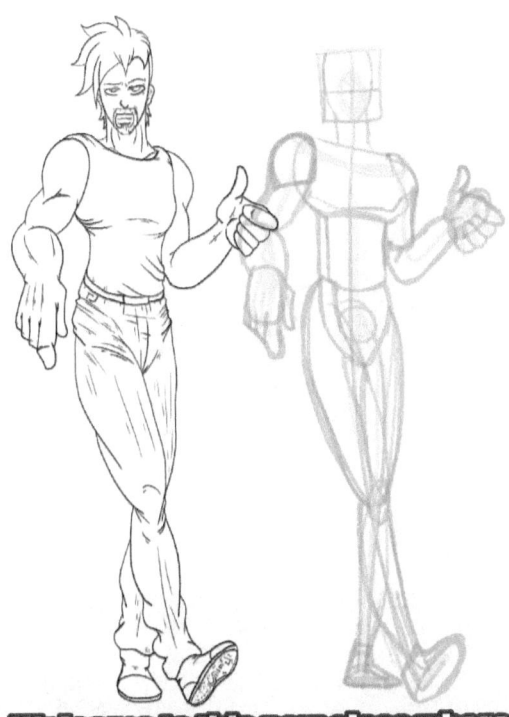

Welcome to this new class where
we will analyze in depth the movement of the figure
and how it is affected by personality and
the character.

It is important to mention that for the correct
application of movement it is necessary to know
thoroughly the structure of the figure, including
of course the human.

We ask you to consult the previous ones or
upcoming manuals and books
of the author that are referring to the drawing for
any doubts about the anatomy.

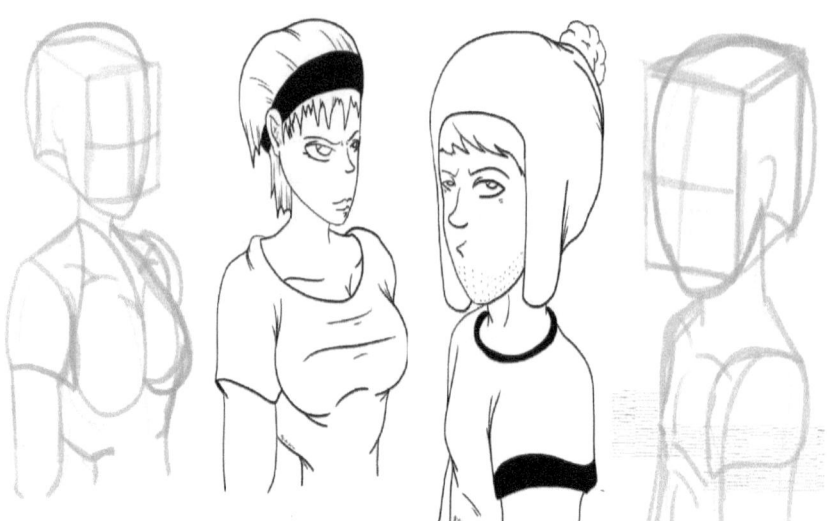

Structure

Remember that the structure is the representation geometric of what we are going to draw. This will define the proportions of the bodies and the volume, remember to use guide lines to take care of the symmetry of the human body and it is important that you locate the midlines of the body, both behind (spine) as in front (chest, abdomen, etc.).

Every style has a different base, however in order to be able to deform the structure as desired the real proportion of the things. Study everything around you and try to visualize its structure.

These are some simple exercises to start using the line of movement. We will begin to form some simple lines of motion.

We start by sketching a little bit to shape to the drawing (do not define!)

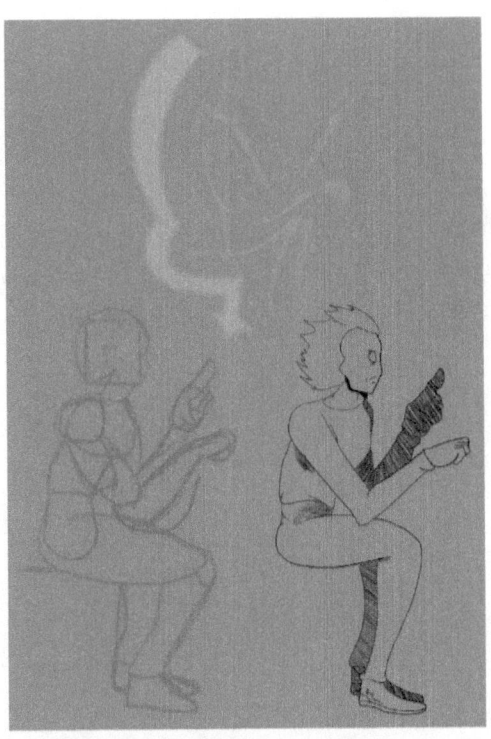

Line of movement

It is the one that gives us the spectacularity
of the movement that we want to represent, or the
apathy of the character.

The line of movement or dynamic line marks the
path that the spine must take and
from it we locate the remaining elements
of the figure: Thorax, Pelvis, etc. Many
sometimes it also marks the correct placement
of the extremities.

In this figure we see a man sitting in profile
where you can see the curvature of the line
of movement giving the feeling of comfort.

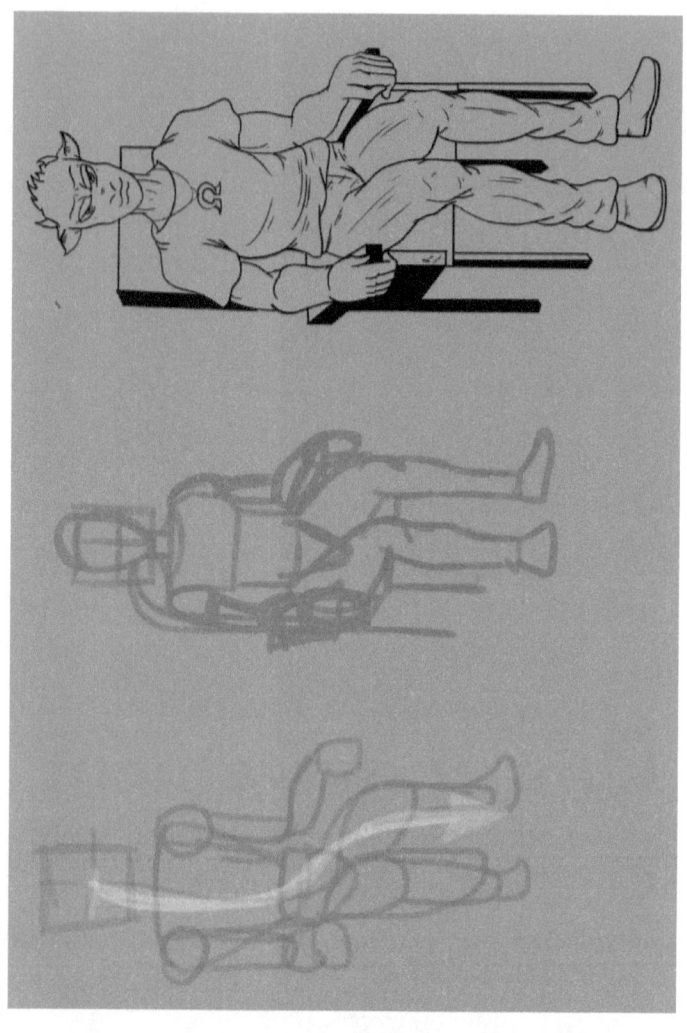

Study this same effect in this 3/4 figure.

It should not be too meandering or so angled, takes into account the movement of the column so you know how far it can go.

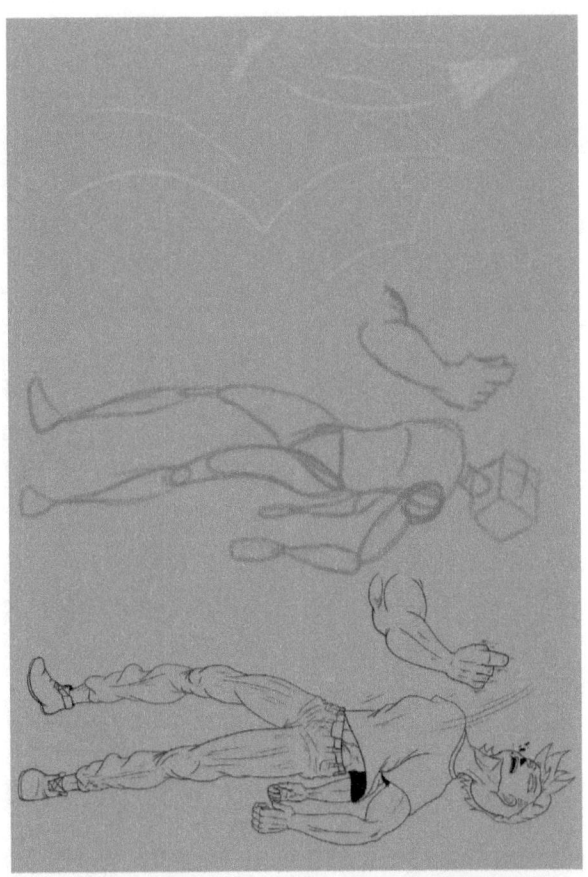

In the superhero comic the spectacularity
is important so all the characters
they must have a different dynamic line, according
to the psychology of the character.

You can use three or four dynamic lines that
mark the action for you. So you have the balance
of the character and his perception.

Here we see an emotionless blow, his line of
movement is not so curved and the impression of the
blow is simplistic.

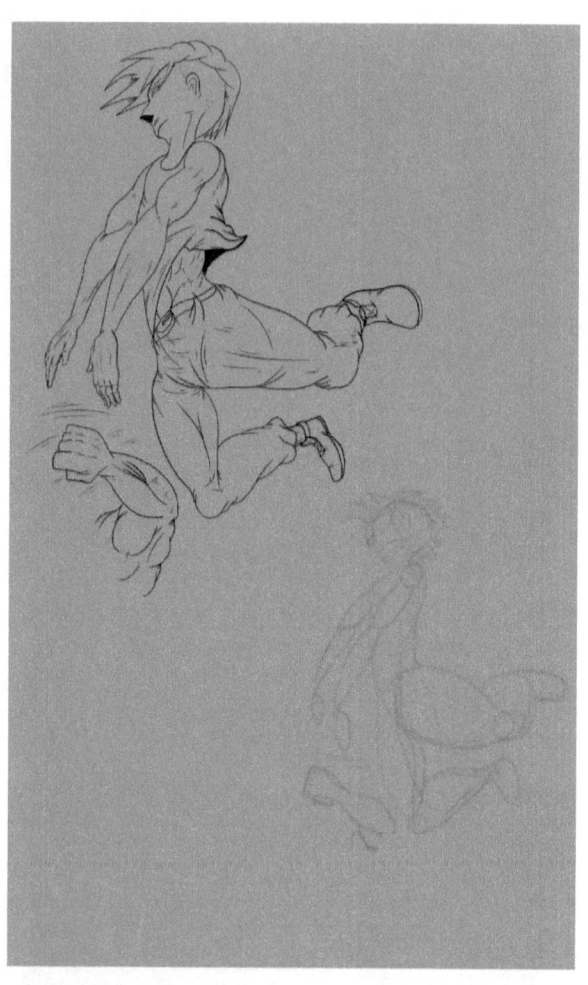

Here, instead we see the same blow but
the line of movement is much more curved,
so the movement action is more striking.

Observe the interaction of arms and legs that
emphasize dynamism.

Now we see a superhero attempt running towards an emergency, the bad thing is that its dynamic line is almost vertical, consequently its movement is very slow and for the action of a super hero no it serves.

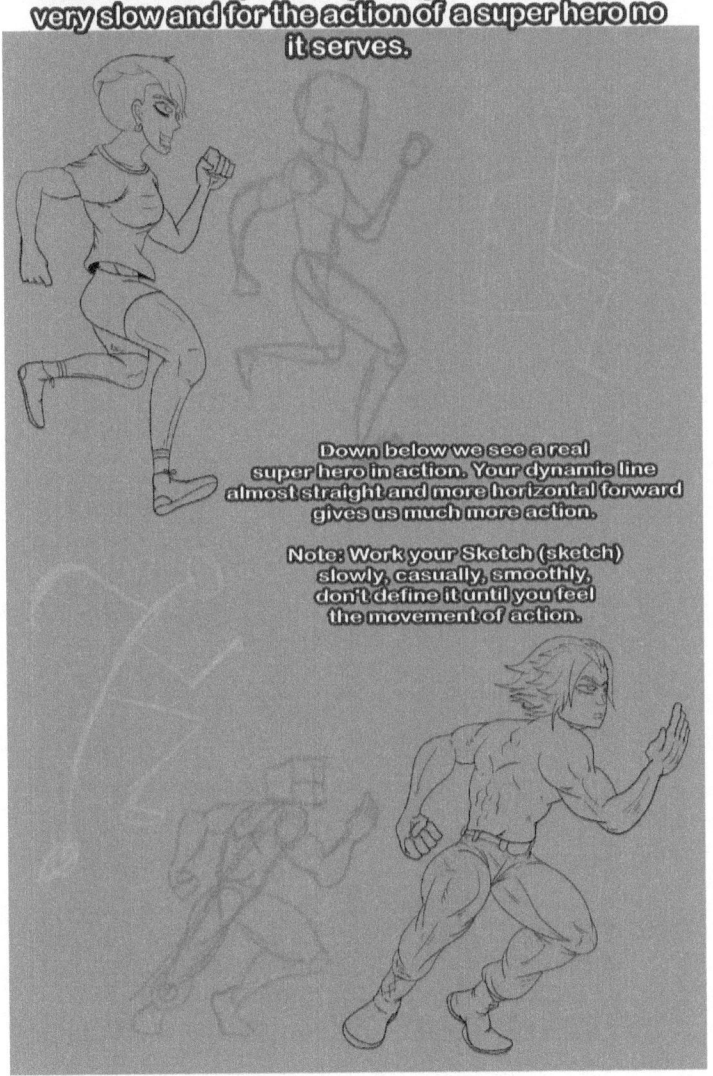

Down below we see a real super hero in action. Your dynamic line almost straight and more horizontal forward gives us much more action.

Note: Work your Sketch (sketch) slowly, casually, smoothly, don't define it until you feel the movement of action.

The line of movement in children is easier, since
they are more carefree and don't bother
do very shocking poses.

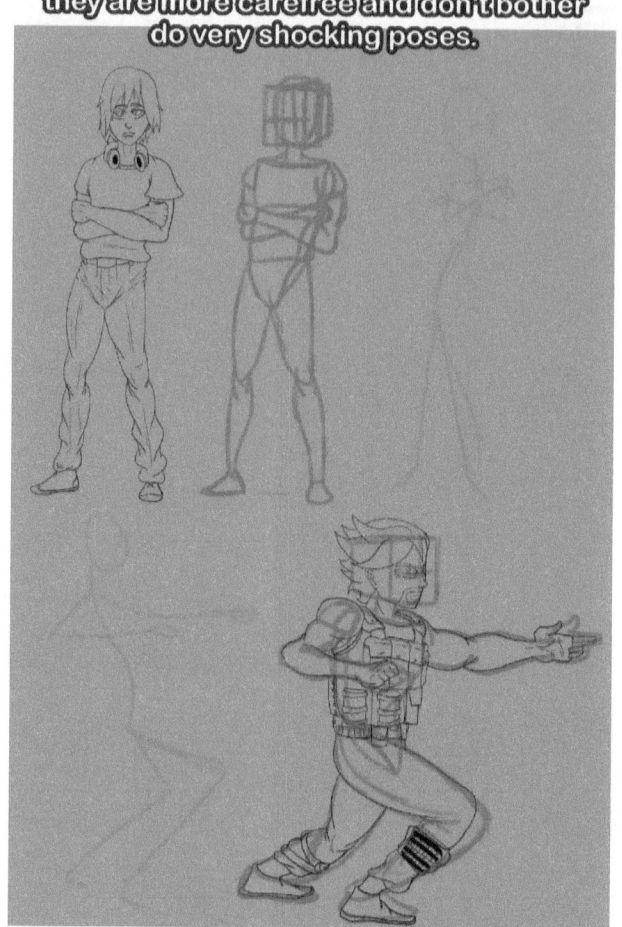

Give the roughest children harder features
and a more aggressive look. Your dynamic line
it is curved, indicating its tendency to
evil, in this case put a beard for
which is not so childish in appearance but this
it serves for immature characters in behavior.

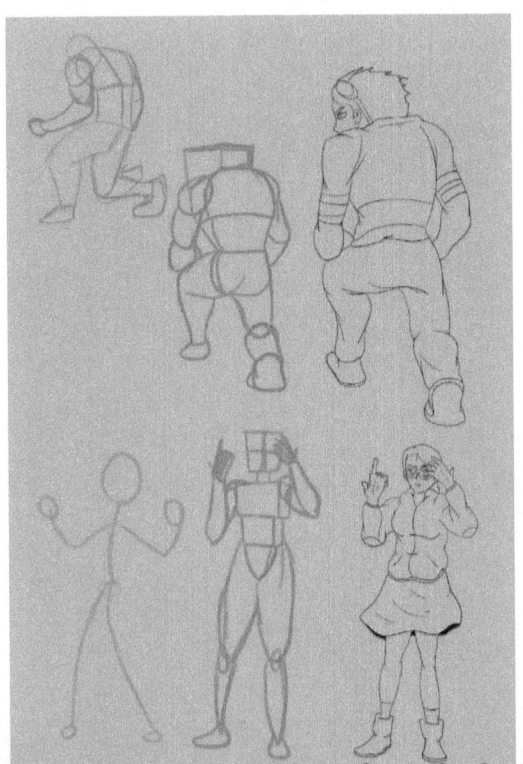

There are different types of children, from the typical nerd to the bullies, passing through the worried ones, the popular, etc.

Check the opposite sides of the attitude in these examples of a child and study how the elements are coupled from the structure to the dynamic line to make your exercises.

Give them typical features like the classic backpack full of books, glasses and school uniform to a guy "Killed" and moves the slightly curved dynamic line to give you the effect of carrying something heavy.

11

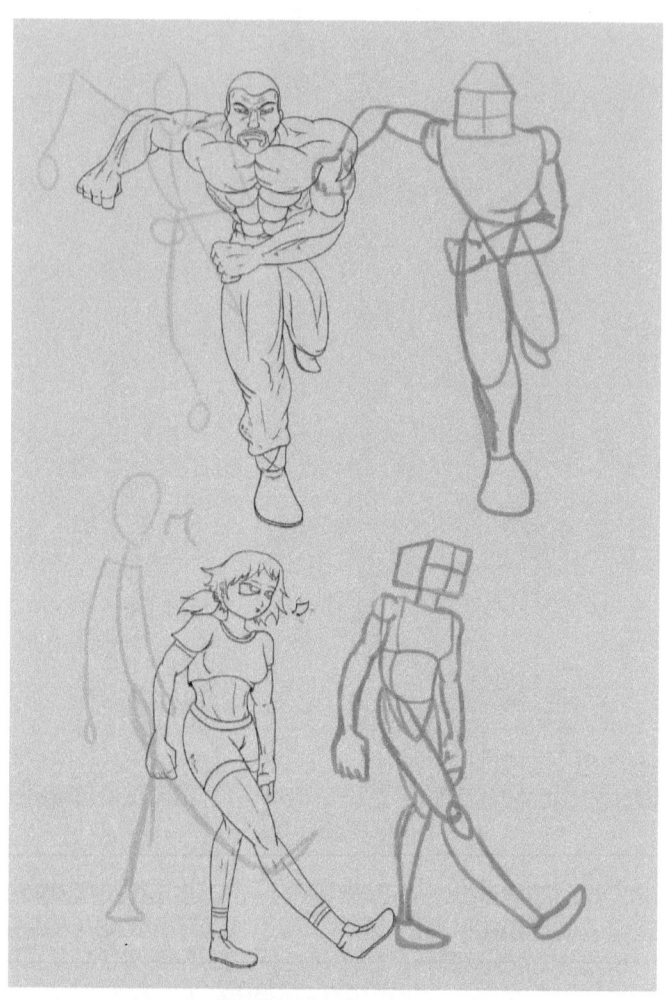

To run, you always lean your body forward to take more speed and the arms move roughly to the sides. instead when we walk carelessly the body rests its weight on legs, slightly arching your back.

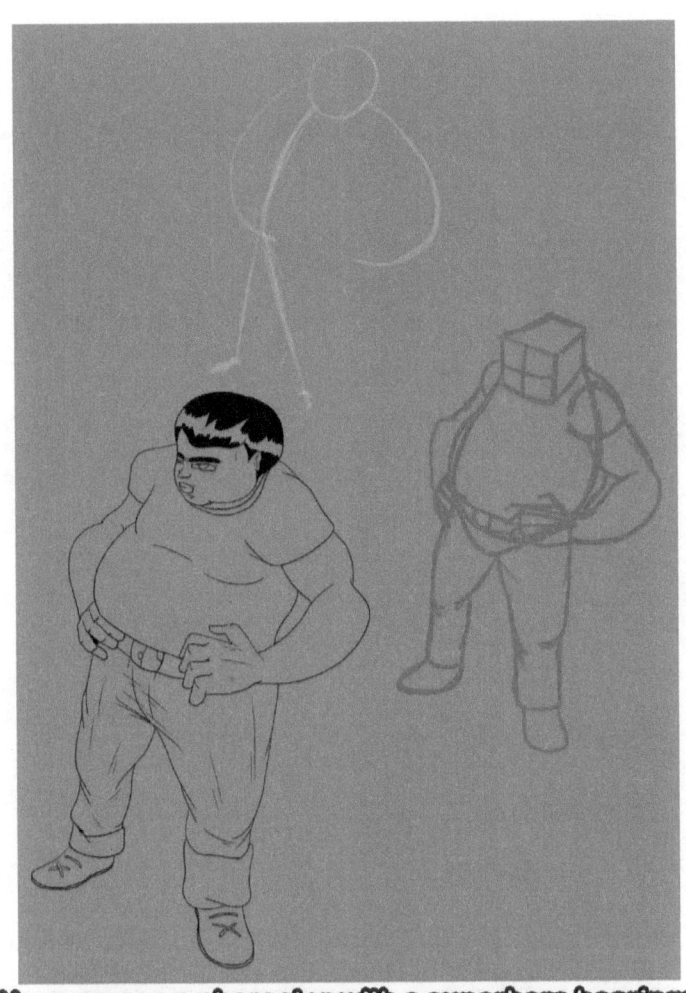

Here we see a character with a superhero bearing:
the pelvis forward, the arms at the waist,
the look of "let's fight for justice"; However,
the volume of his body and style of clothing
invariably like a kid who defends his
companions and friends of the bad guys.

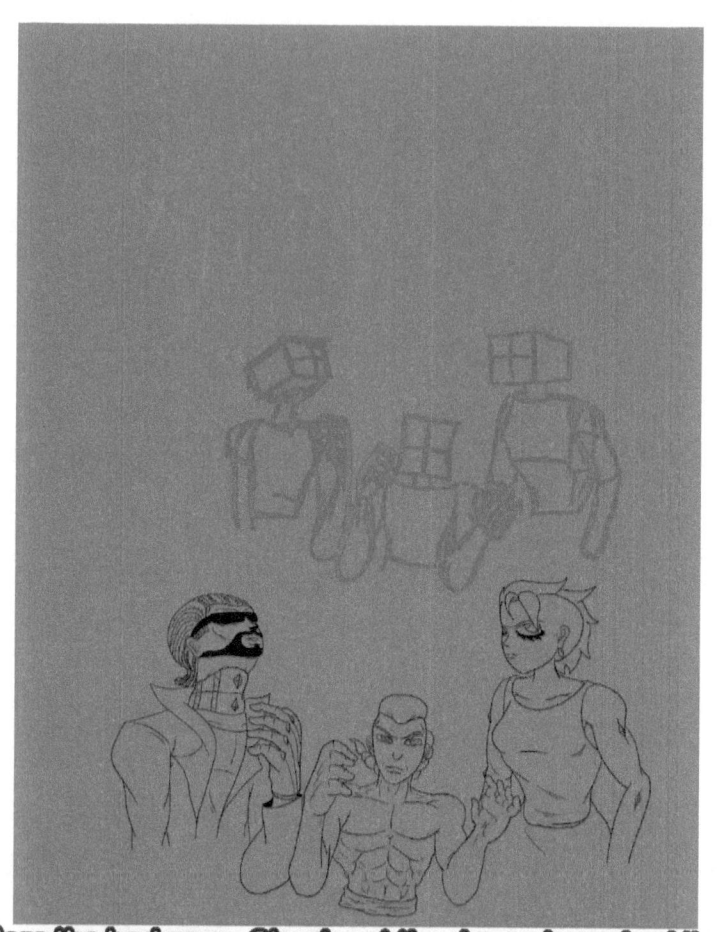

Here the bad guys. Check out the dynamic arched line
in all three, the detail of the lower jaws very
big and leaning forward it gives them a touch of
childish evil and individual characteristics
like haircut, clothes, look and volume
His body highlights his "evil" personality.
The hands give more realism to the attitude, not
forget it

14

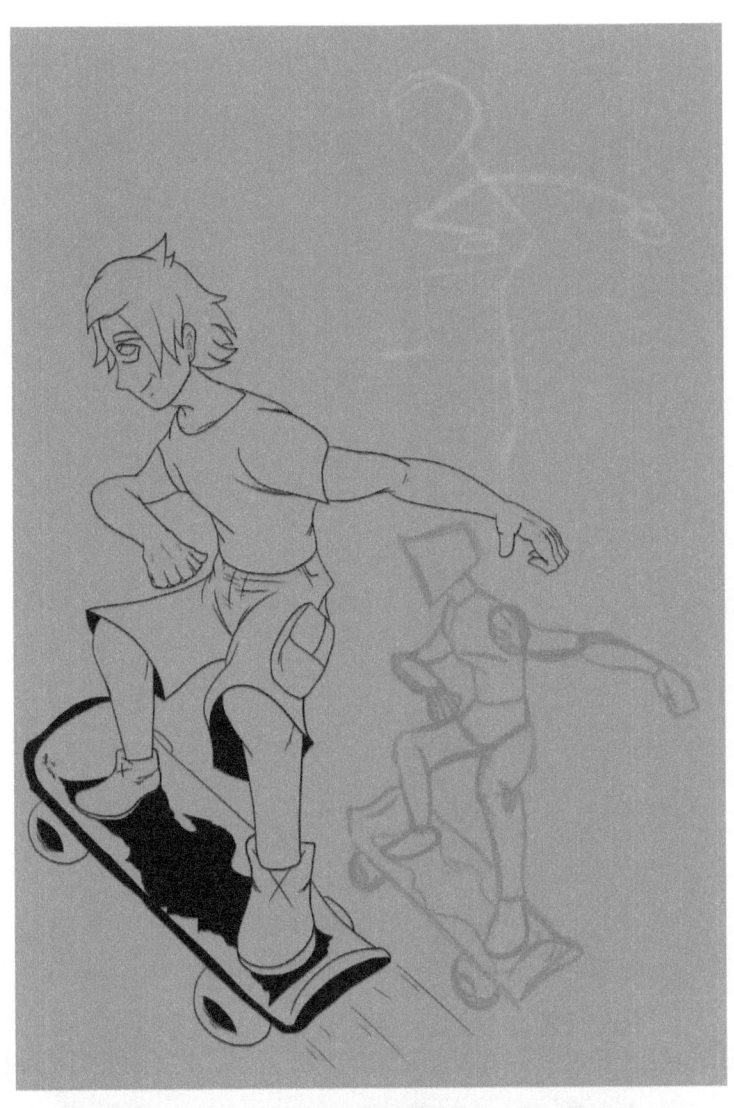

On the contrary, sporty children have a line straighter dynamics, which gives us the idea of more vitality.

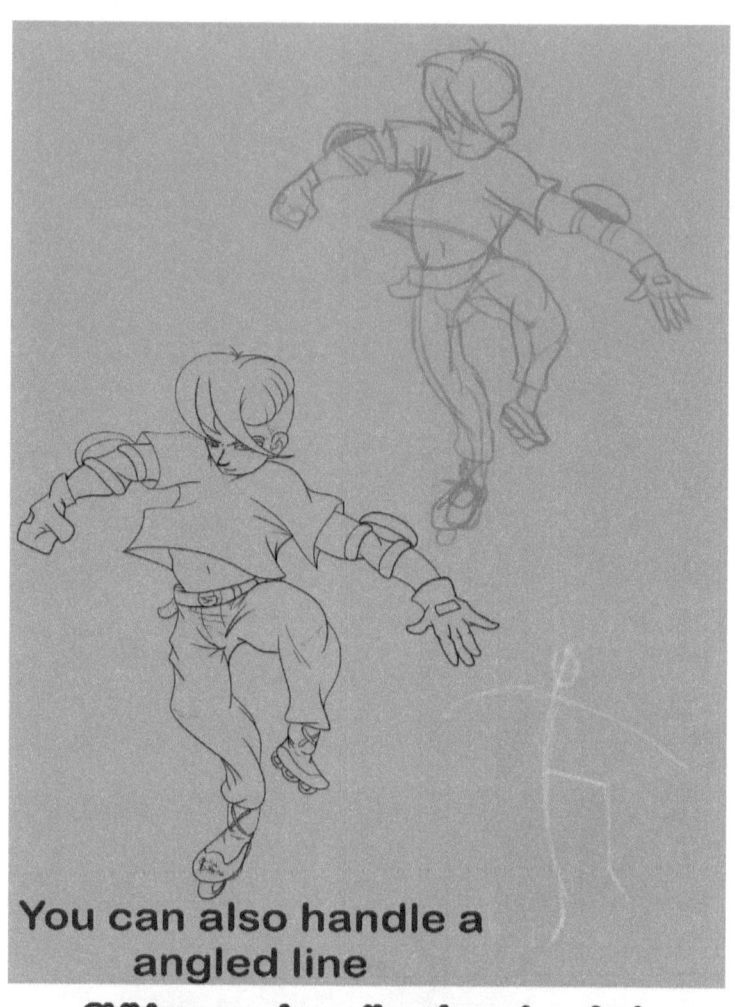

You can also handle a angled line

Children are also action characters, just
that the action does not involve explosions, shootings or
sexy girls in evening dresses ... how about a good
board or skates that imbue speed to actions.
Of course, with due protection so that none
get hurt.

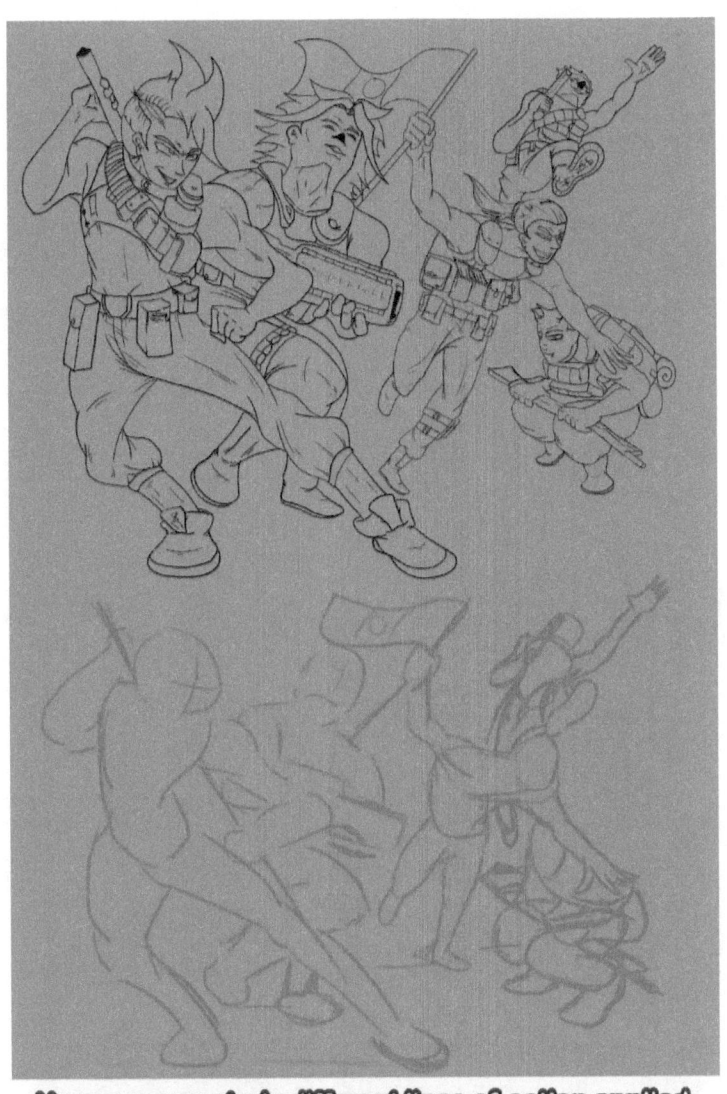

Here you can study different lines of action applied
to a single drawing. Check the patterns or the type of clothing
to detail your characters.

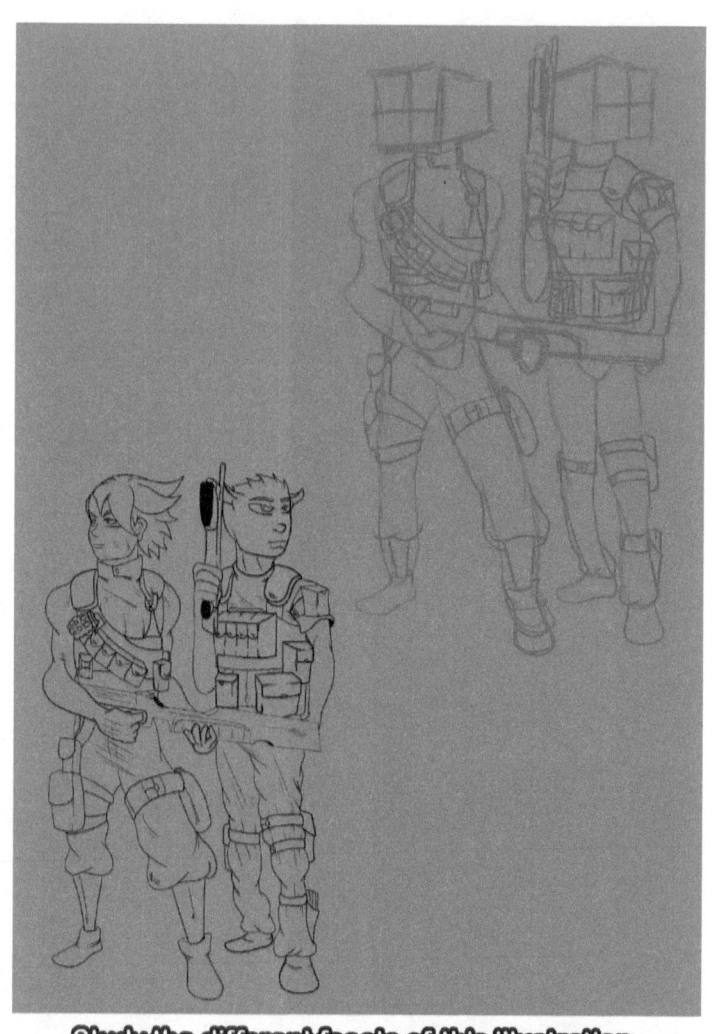

Study the different facets of this illustration,
both the individual structure as a whole, the dynamism
of each character and the orientation of the whole illustration in
general and check the difference between the pencil finish and
in ink.

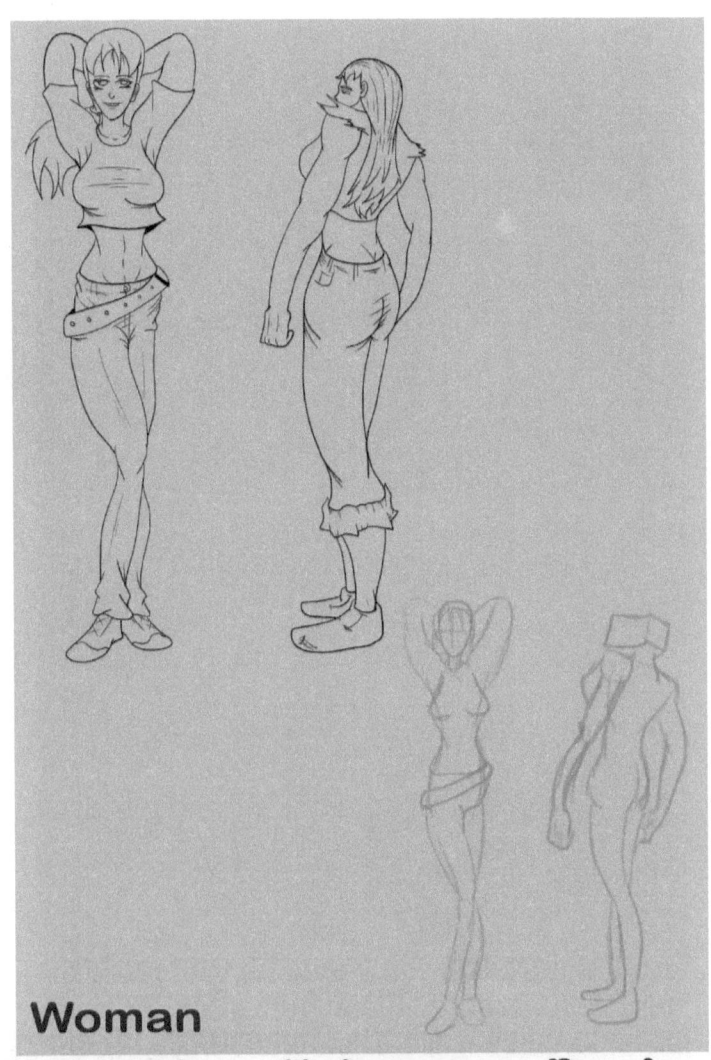

Woman

Women are drawn with sinuous curves, if you draw
The curved line of movement makes the woman look
sexier. In addition, the waist and the
hip break so characteristic in women.

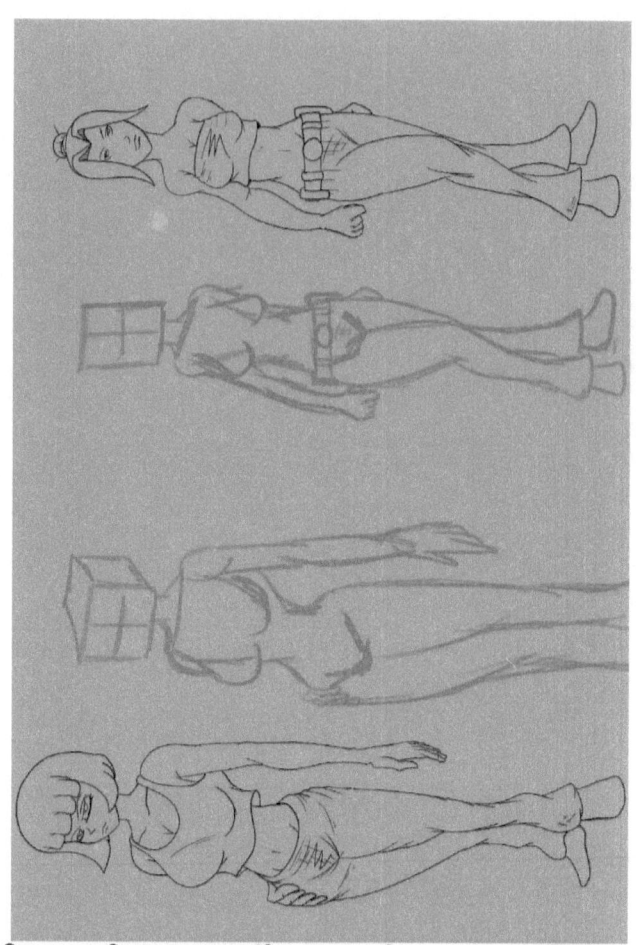

Among how sexy they can be, women have different personalities: Fatals, tender Girls, Heroines, Villains, Nerds, Casual Girls, Etcetera.

Let's analyze the different types and their dynamics, so that have a great variety when creating your own characters.

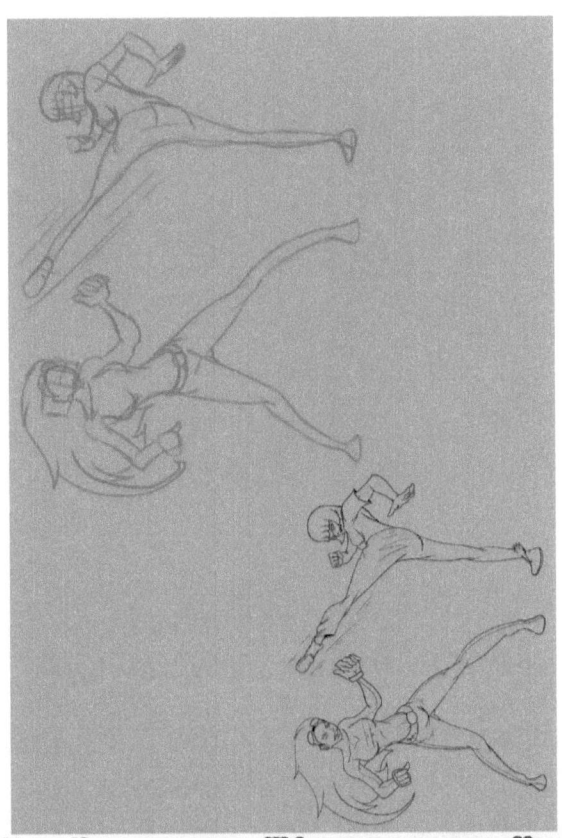

An attractive woman will be even more attractive if
she is a woman of action. Study in these examples some
very flexible dynamic lines for super
heroine and a fighter.
Check that although they keep their bearing sexy,
their strength and character are more marked.

Don't forget that depending on the characteristics
of the characters, will be the details that
reaffirm.

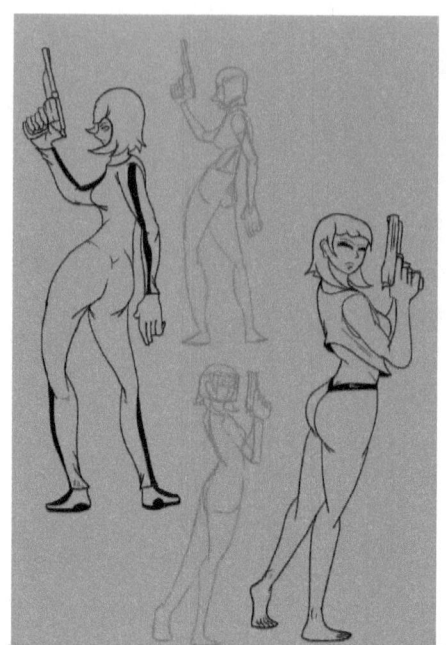

Let's now look at some types of girls.

We have here two girls in arms, but with marked differences between them.

Villains usually look rough and difficult to correct and his features are more sullen.

Heroic women show serenity on their faces and patience.

As they are women who are in constant action, they must have clothing that doesn't get in the way, either in a latex suit or a mini blouse and underwear. The women of action rarely wear baggy clothes.

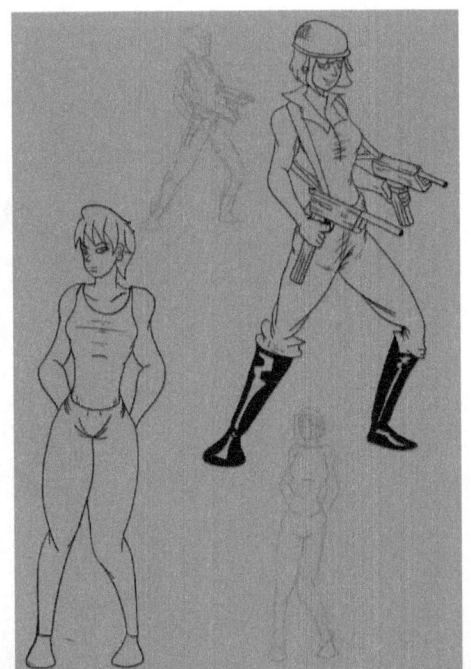

Let's study these contrasts of personality in women
They are highlighted by their actions and clothing.

On the one hand, we have a villain armed to the teeth.
His features are hard and he always frowns.

On the other, we see a tender, almost childish girl with features
very soft, big eyes, casual clothes and short hair.

Her attitude between tender and innocent contrasts
with the ways of his body, which makes it look very nice.

Observe the dynamic lines of both: a very angled one
and with great force, the other much more curved and flexible.
Have note that depending on the dynamic line that from the
principle, your drawing will have the finish you want.

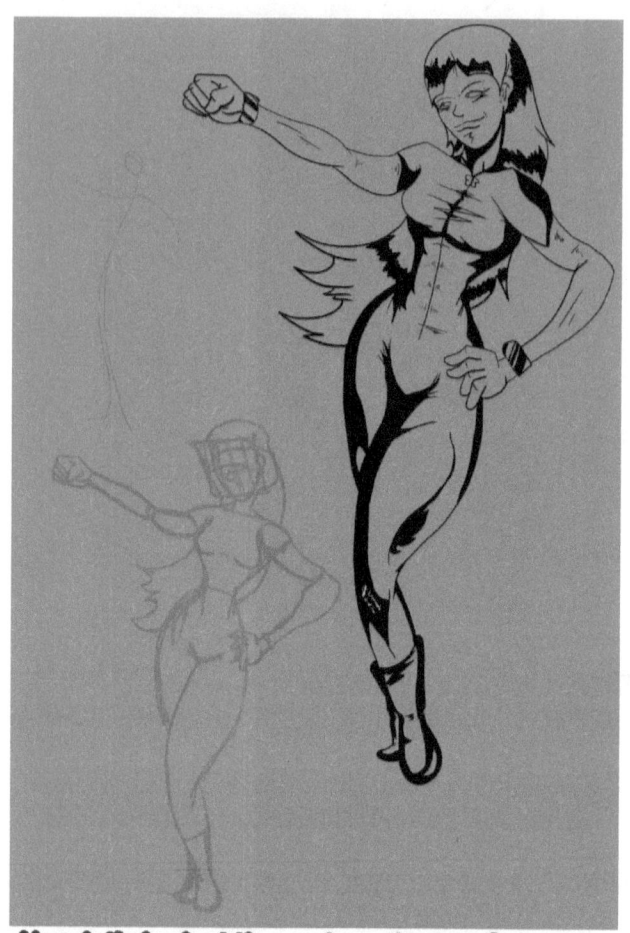

Now let's look at three stereotypes of women:

Villain: With a curved dynamic line, it maintains a sexy pose, but her face and attitude tell us how bad it can be. Wear practical clothing that denotes his strength to use it when necessary.

You can hide all kinds of things in your suit.

24

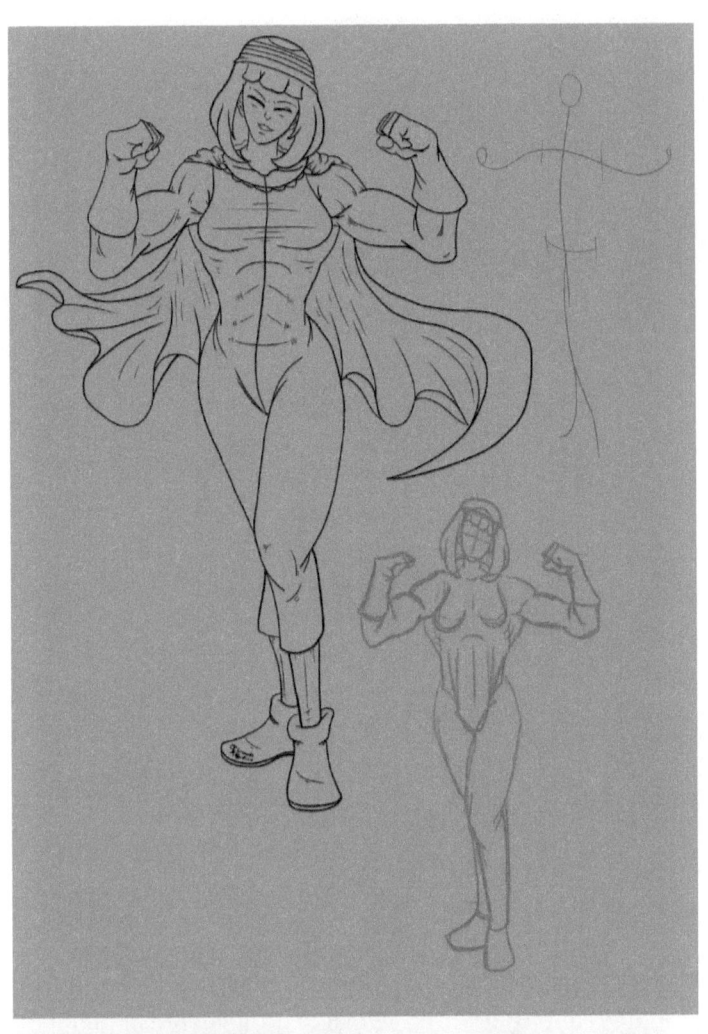

The Heroine: With impressive pose and serene face
and friendly, wear a cape that denotes your quality of
bravery and uses nothing but his strength and intelligence
to fight evil. The dynamic line too
it is sexy with a certain touch of superiority.

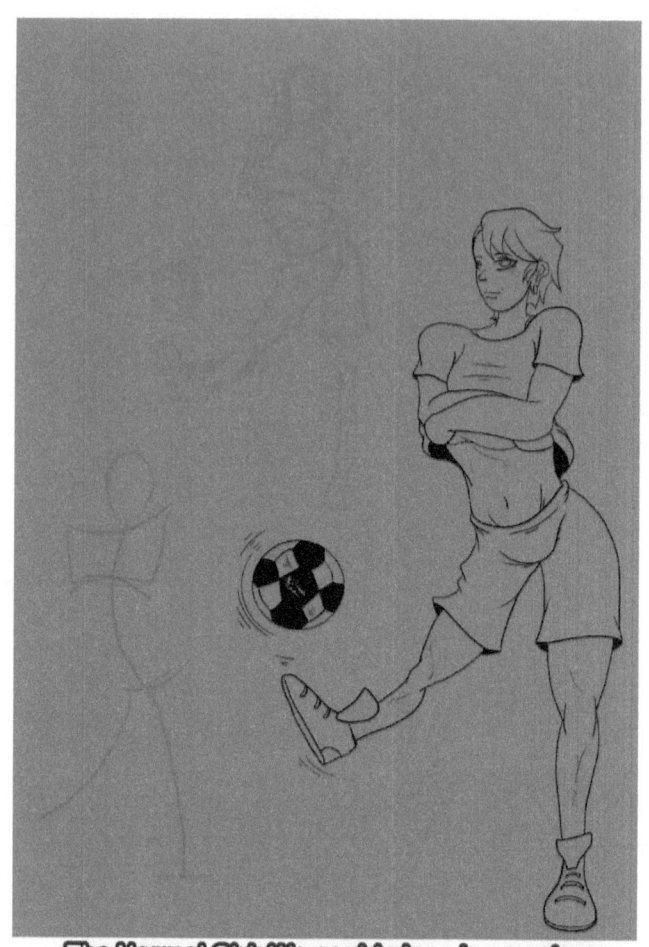

The Normal Girl: We could place in any story
and it would look good, it's a sketch of what it could be
a good character. Here we see her in a sporting stage,
with his bermuda, his shirt and his ball, although perfectly
we could dress her in any way.

Study the "static" line of movement that helps us,
Although the girl is standing idle, she looks dynamic.

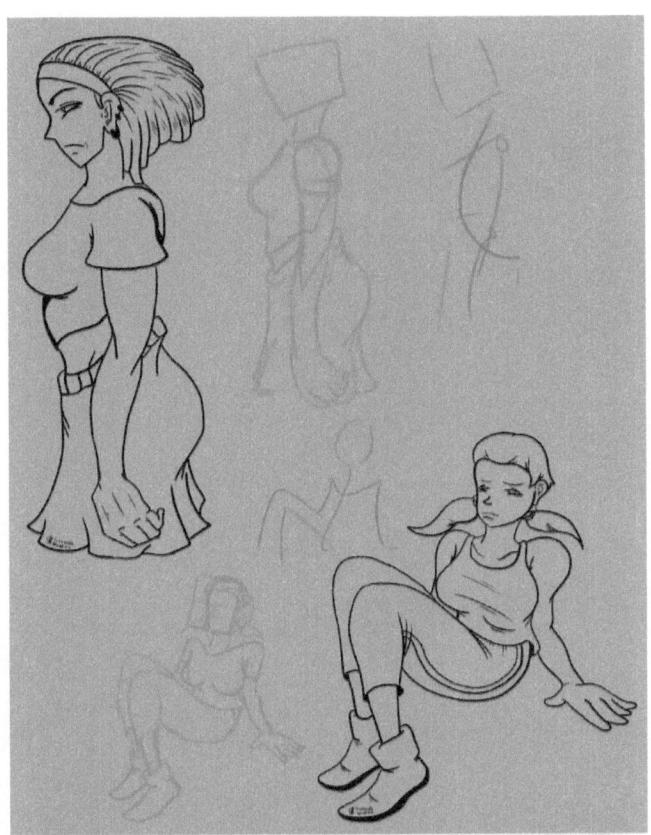

The line of movement also marks our personality.
Look at these two different attitudes and the structures of each
one, as an exercise try to draw each of these girls
with the attitude of another, that is, draw the girl from the
dreadlocks very thoughtful and conversely with each other.

See also the details in the clothing that reinforces
the importance of each character: For example, the girl
Rastafarian could be a co-star or even the character
main story. The sitting girl could be an extra
or the friend of some protagonist.

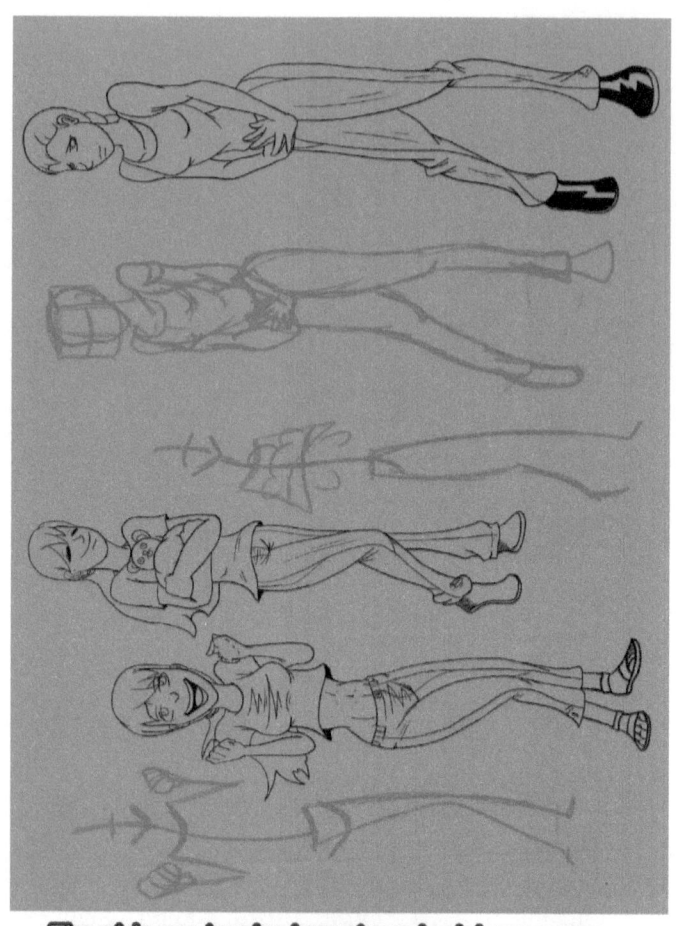

The girls are tender by nature, look here some
of his classic reactions. The dynamic line is important
do not forget.

When designing a character, you must give it consistent attitudes
with his personality although you can play with the poles
opposites, experiment creating a girl of appearance
tender, but with a murderous character.

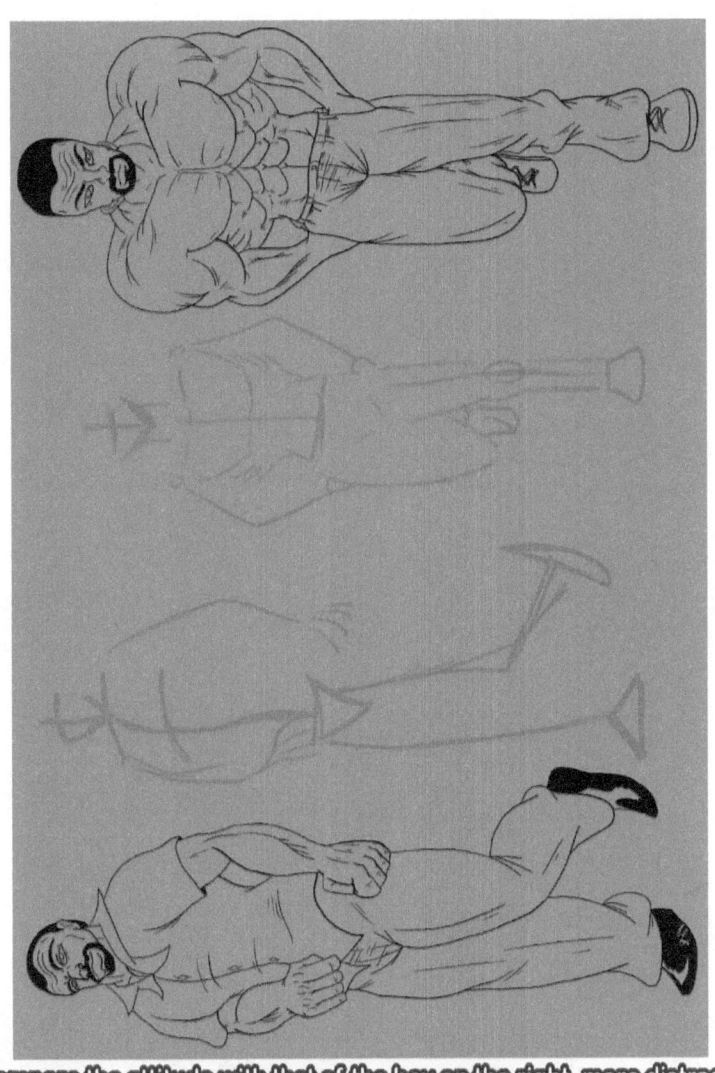

Compare the attitude with that of the boy on the right, more distracted and shy, typical of a man.

Or, on the contrary, happy and good-natured.

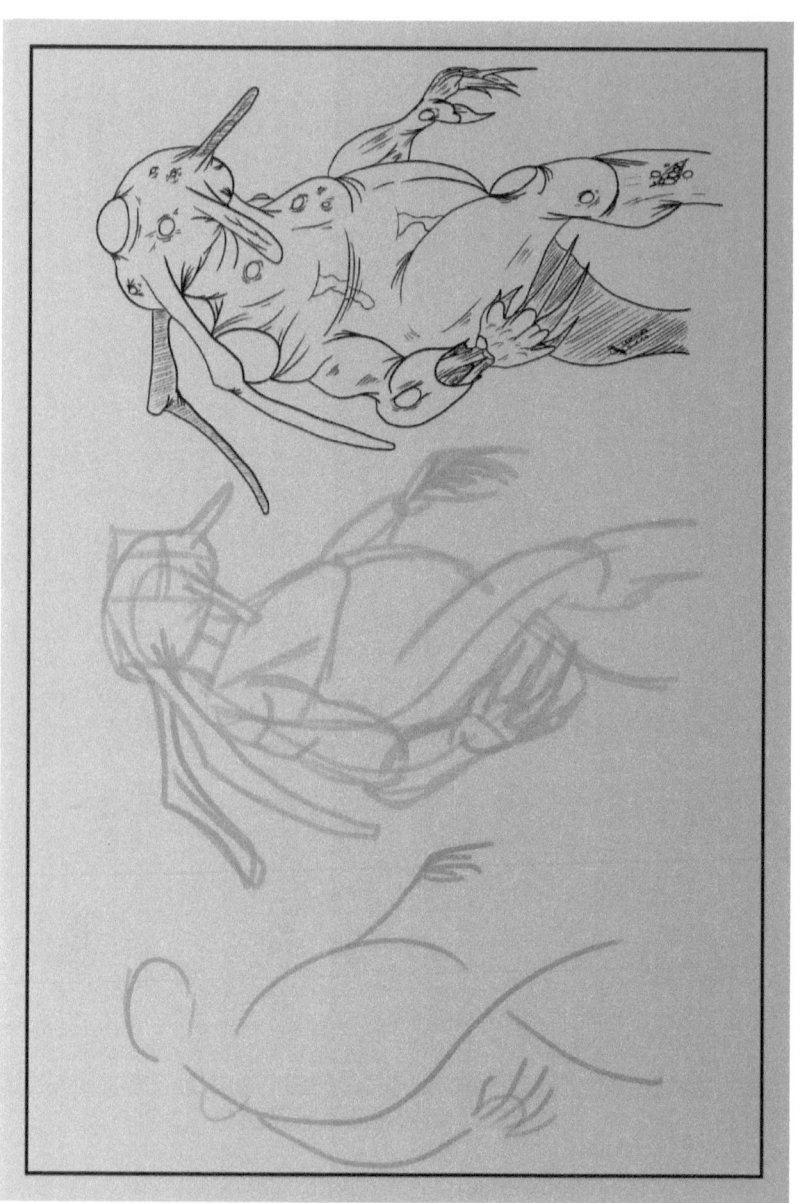

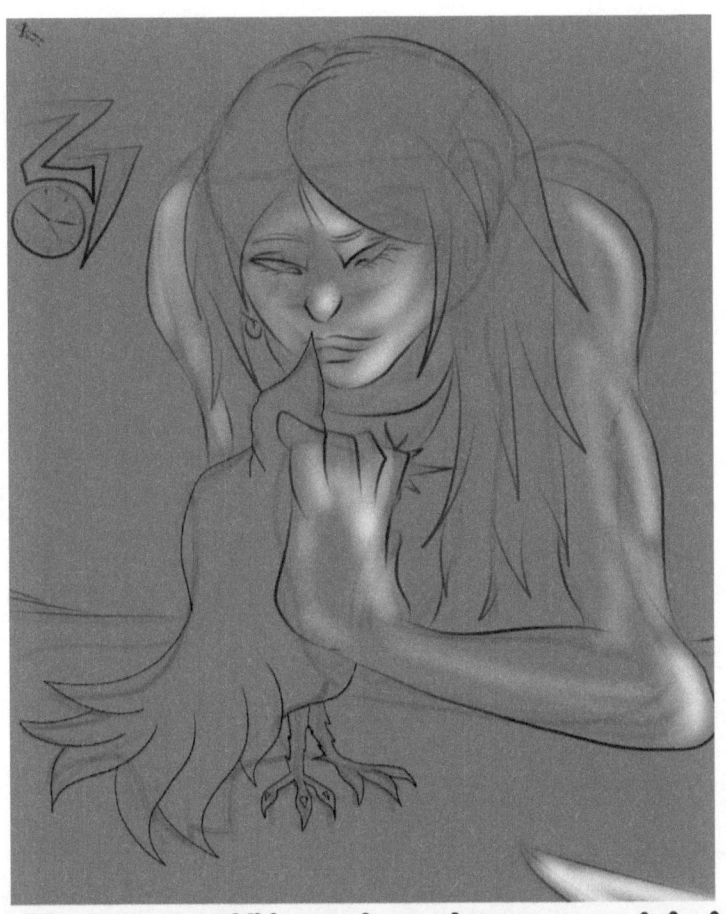

In addition to women, children and super heroes you must also learn to create less typical people and to give more variety to your stories. Deform the actual proportions to create characters fat, skinny, deformed, etc.

See how the proportions are deformed to form bodies of different kinds. With your arms down below your knees, very short or very skinny legs.

31

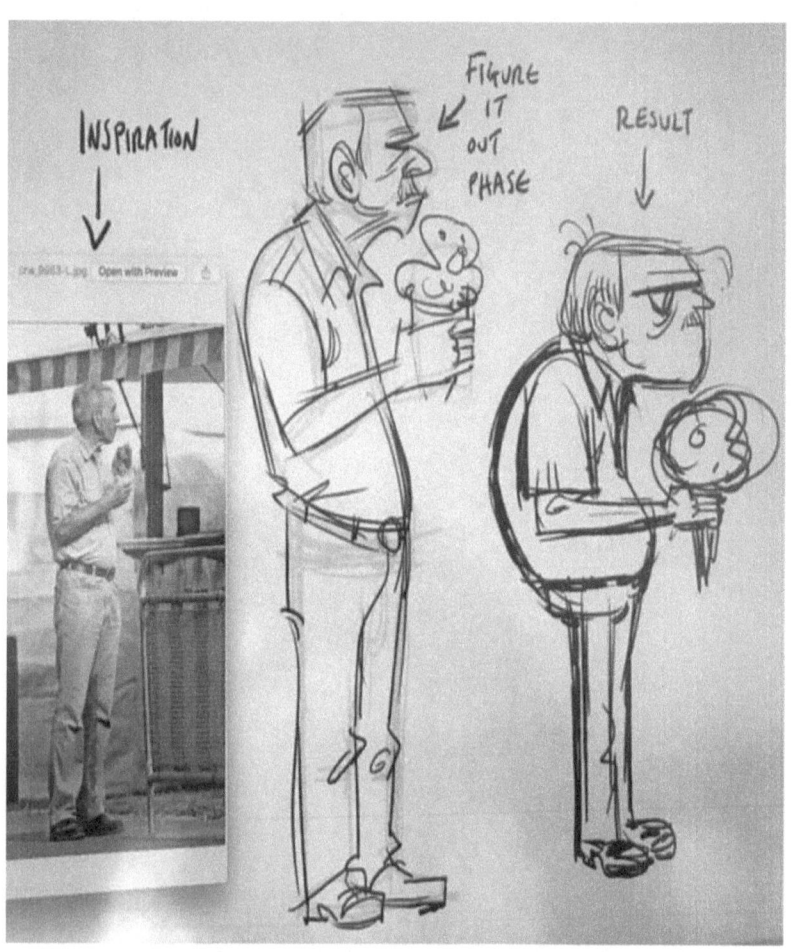

Practice the structures of people of different ages and complexions.

The walking of the elderly is usually slow, calm,
accompanied by its smooth line of movement, with the back
slightly hunched over the years, look at the details
from the face in the figure above to draw an older person.

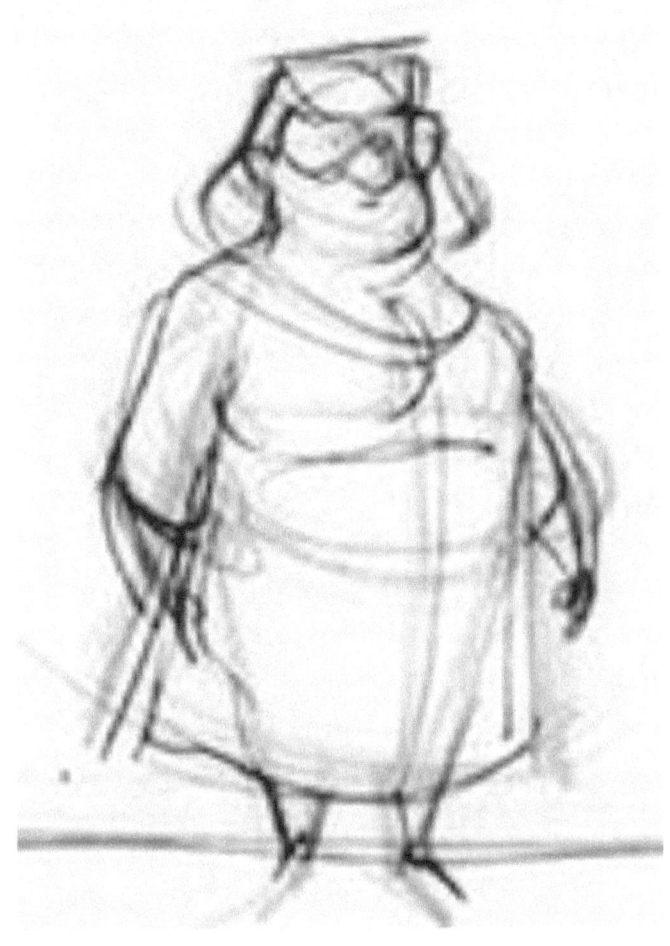

On the contrary, a neighbor lady is disheveled, angry, grumbles about everything and has strong arms or excessive force from so much washing. The tubes in the hair although optional are another characteristic feature.

See that his gills are too pronounced.

33

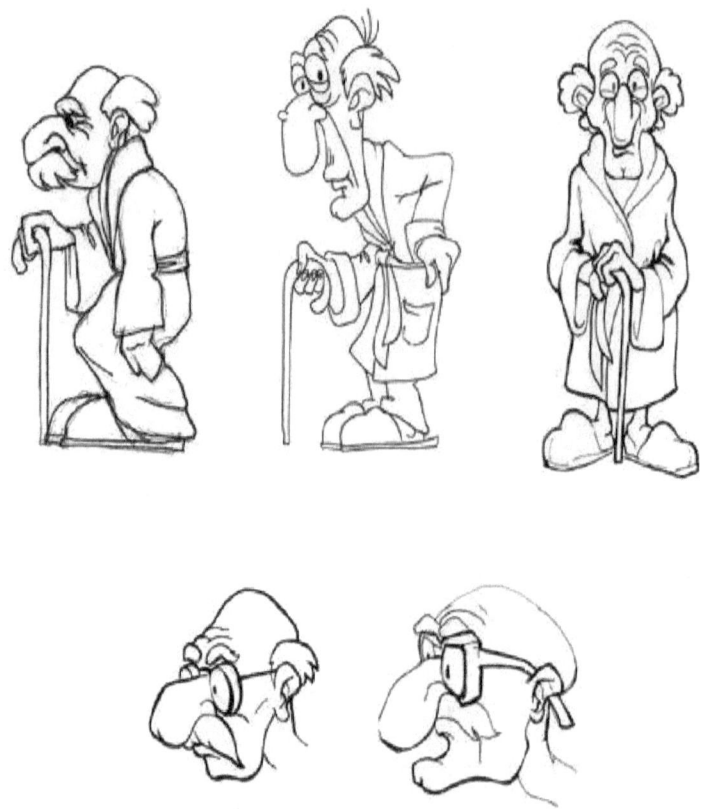

Now, a bossy old man, yelling at all the people and ordering them.

The dynamic line is also curved, but is supported by a secondary element: the cane. The lack of teeth and the smile teasing give us an idea of the type of person he is.

34

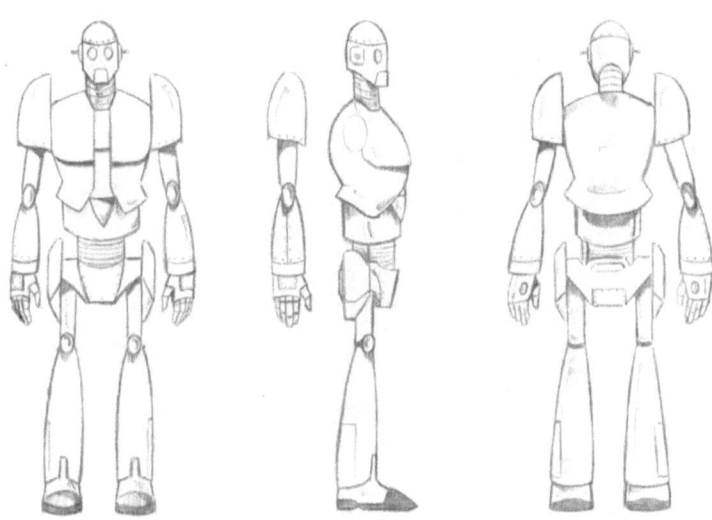

You can also create mechanical designs (or mecha).

When you design mecha you will realize that the drawing of the basic structure will help you a lot, because the joints of a robot are like the structure of the human figure.

Depending on the design of the wick, we can know if this serve good or evil. Try to handle red and black tones in evil robots and blue or white in good ones.

Place the logos that identify the creator somewhere or the shield of his side.

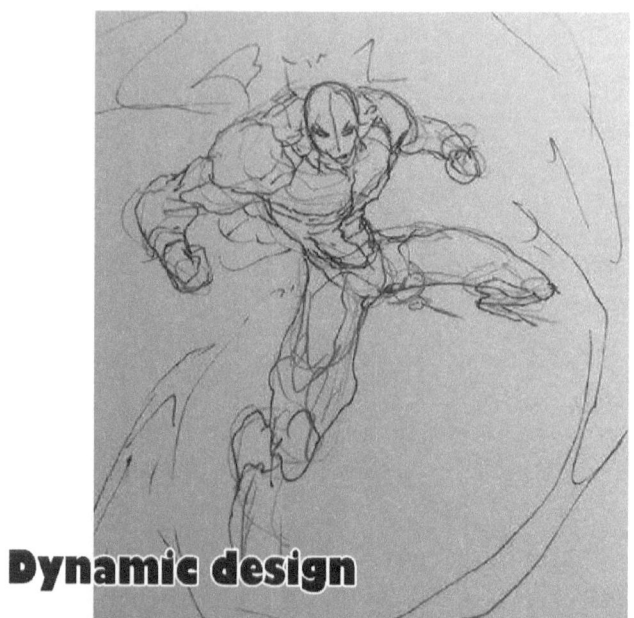

Dynamic design

To design a character we must handle all aspects well
of it, starting with the writing, which will give us an idea of
personality, appearance, and finally the genre of it.

Suppose having our script (written definition of a
character or work), we must design a space guardian who protects
a far quadrant of the inhabited planets, use a photon weapon
to ignite aliens and always helps navigators in
misfortune.

Ok, the first thing is to give an image to our guardian. It must be a type
weird, very serious, but to some extent friendly, let's take into account
who lives far from people, which makes him a lonely person.
Now ... he's a space guardian, so he must have a suit
that molds to your anatomy so that it allows you to hit the villains
No problem. You must also wear a helmet. Because maybe ours
character breathes oxygen and in the open space there is not much.

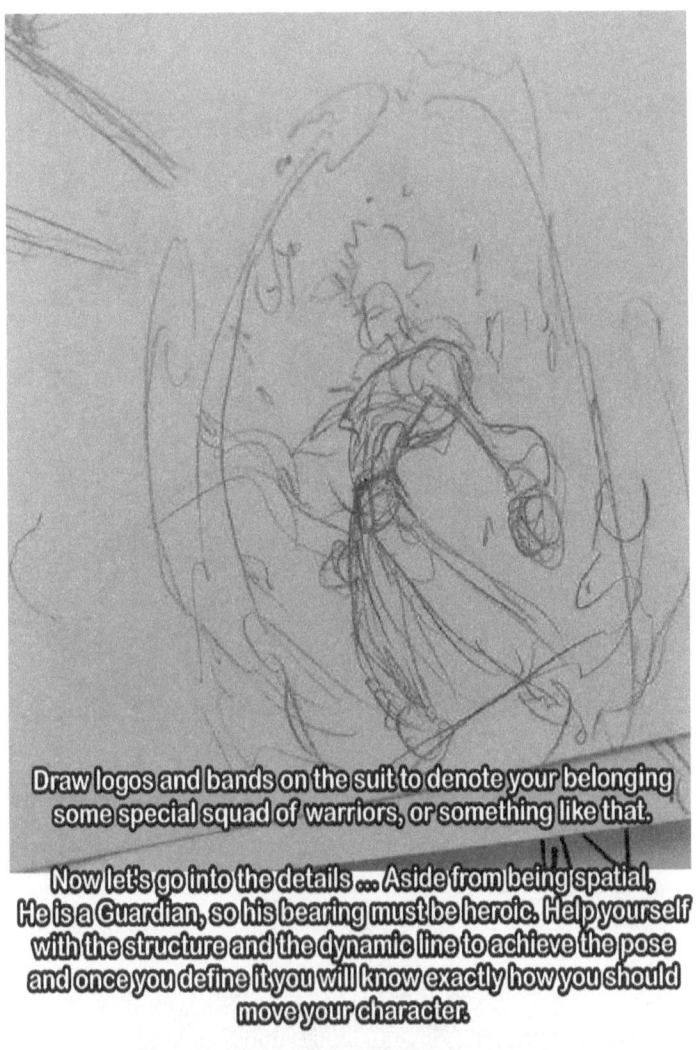

Draw logos and bands on the suit to denote your belonging some special squad of warriors, or something like that.

Now let's go into the details ... Aside from being spatial, He is a Guardian, so his bearing must be heroic. Help yourself with the structure and the dynamic line to achieve the pose and once you define it you will know exactly how you should move your character.

Important details like "rivets" on the base the hull of the leg must be removed from the Script.

Do not forget the design of the weapon, remember that it is photon.

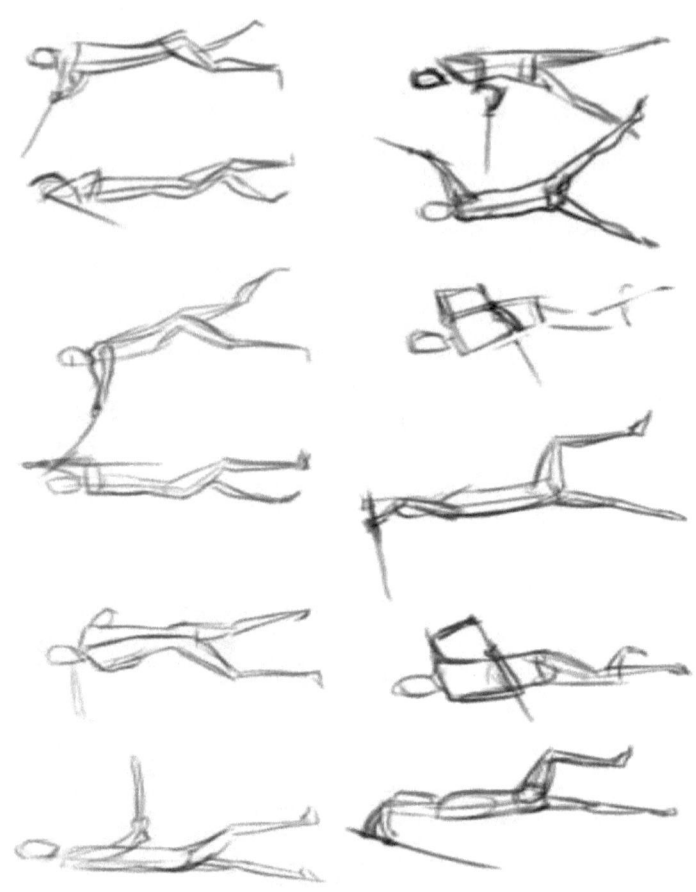

So we can give life to countless characters. A giant enemy, leader of a clan who wishes to dominate the inhabited colonies around, for example. Remember that the first part is the written part and, from this, we work on the graph, later we will see the development of a hero and a villain. Don't forget the dynamic line and the coupling of the different structures on it.

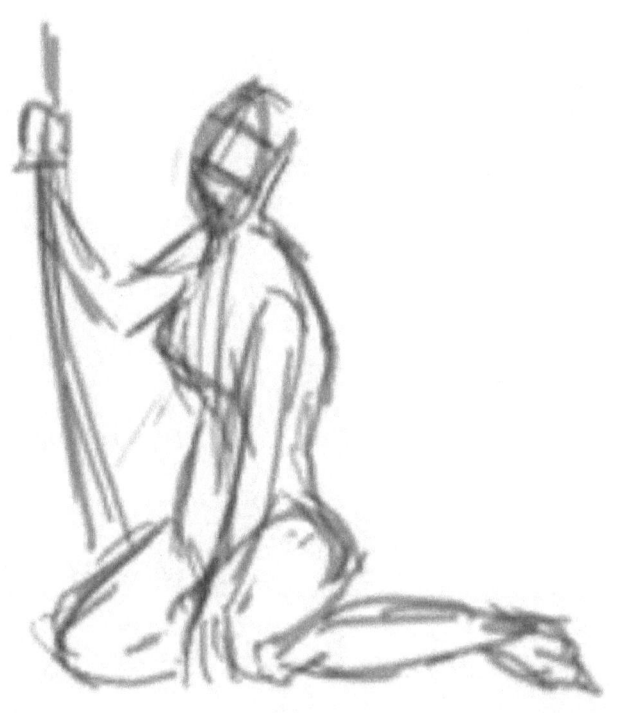

We can also create some characters that live with him
in its history. His partner (and patiño), the inexperienced young man who
you want to be like the superhero and that maybe in future chapters
become your enemy.

The villain of history, a legendary alien who trapped
in the body of a child has lowered the level of its power to the degree
of not being able to get out of it, although not because of it is less
Machiavellian. Counterpart of our space guardian, you not only
want to dominate inhabited colonies, but the entire universe ...
When you leave the body that has.

39

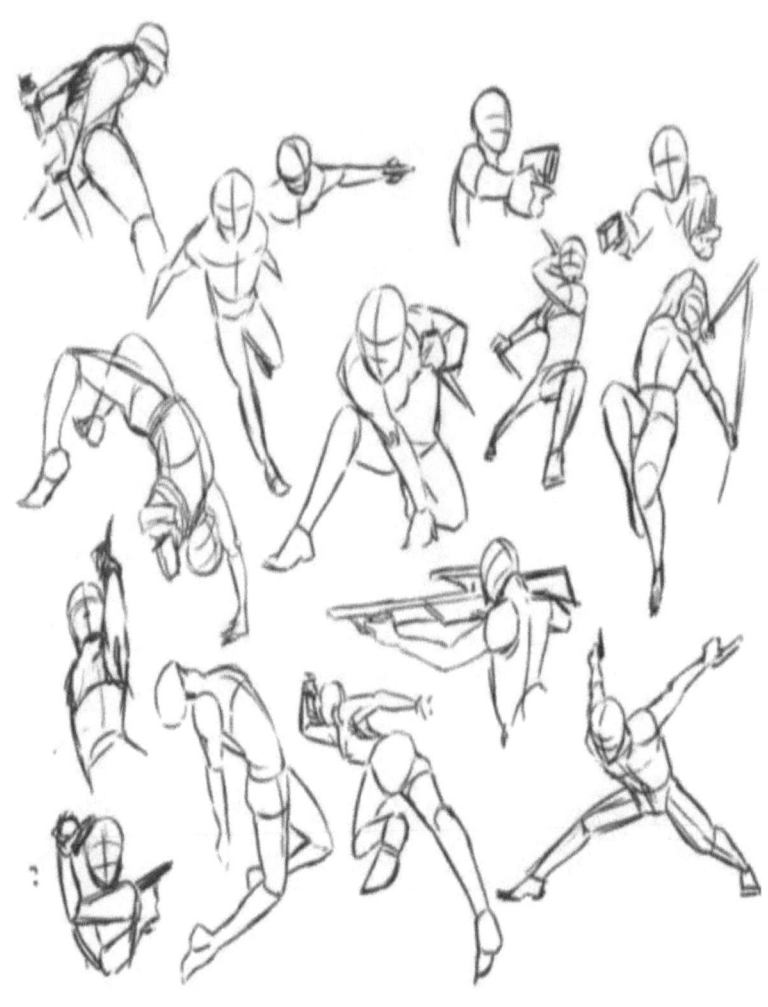

There are also mercenary demons that help the best bidder and are the comedians of the series. They can in one or two chapters help the hero.

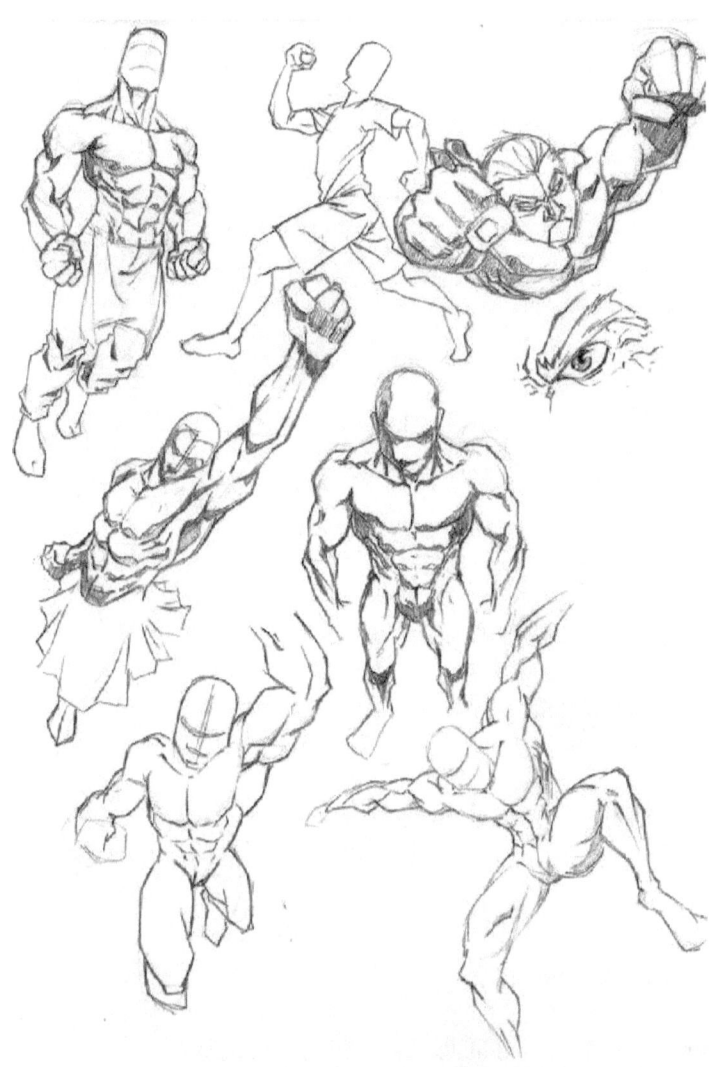

And we cannot miss the teacher of our hero, chief cleric of the inhabited colonies in which all the people have deposited their confidence and that in the end he will be the traitor and the meanest of all the history.

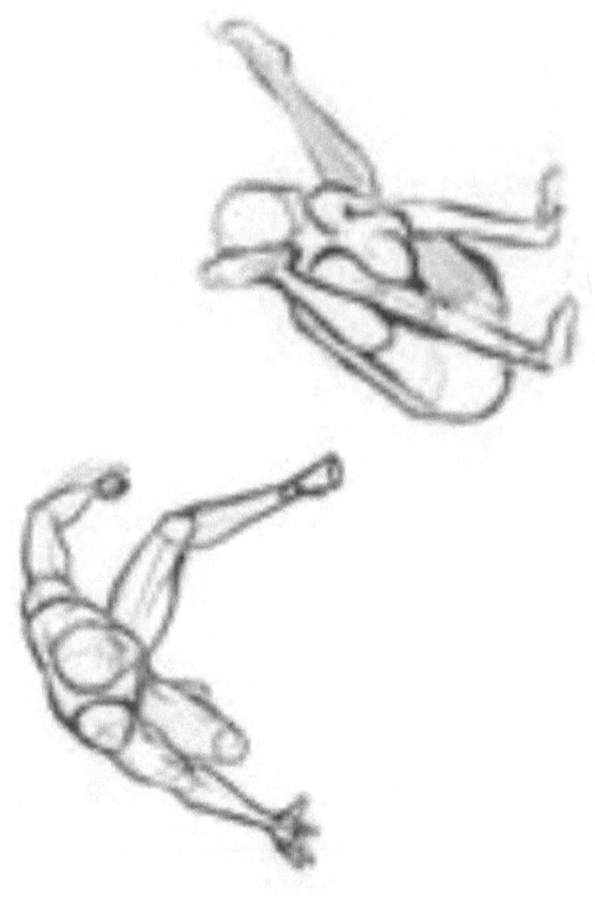

Also create different races of creatures like demons or classes
of aliens as well even the head of the space squad has no
than necessarily being human.

Study the lines of action and the different structures of these
characters, practice with your own creations and invent everything
what you wish.

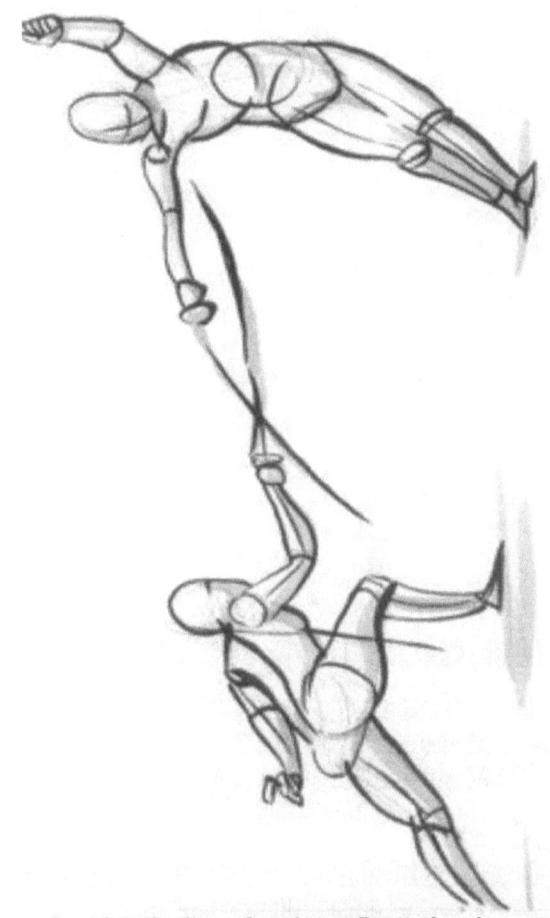

Remember that the line of action reflects the character of our character, if they are very elastic, very serious, very strong, very fat people, etc. It is the basis of our character, the basis of dynamism.

And as the base, the detail is also important, it gives characteristics unique to our characters and fills them with life.

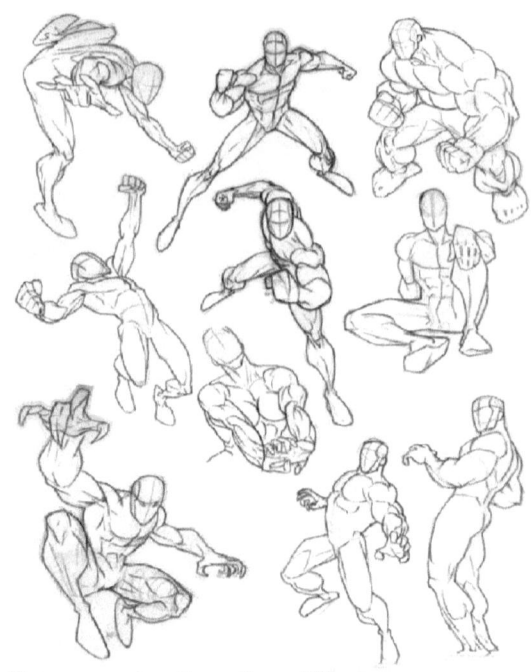

Development of a Hero

In superhero comics, the hero is the biggest part
important. Superheroes are the stereotype of the perfect man.
Handsome, Big, Strong, Muscular, although not always
they are popular.

They have a secret identity that protects their relatives and
friends of the evil attack.

They are gentle with the ladies, but rough with the bad guys and maybe
have some childhood trauma, they spend worrying
for the others, even if they are kicking, they are also
aware that "great power always involves great
responsibility".

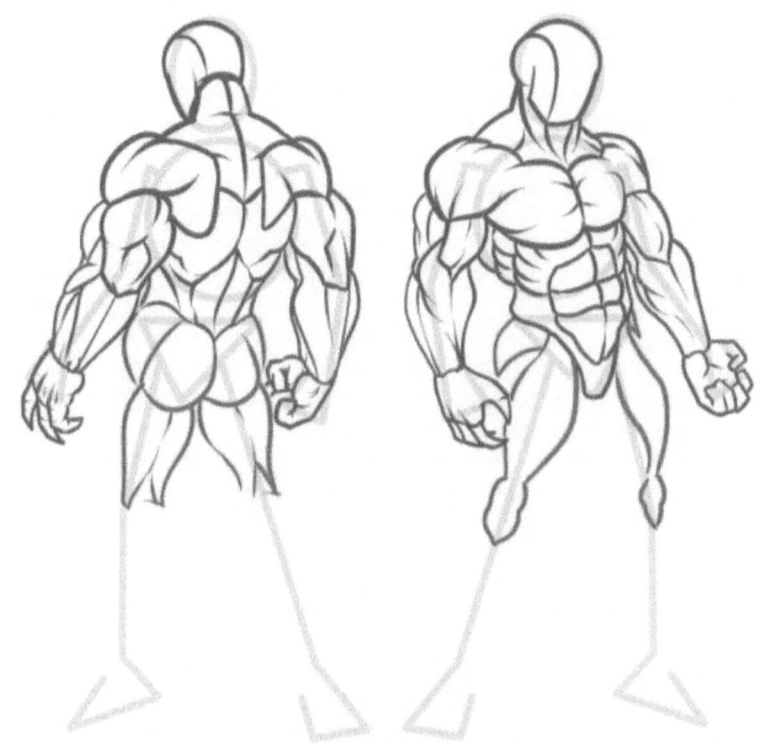

The superhero's demeanor is dynamic, athletic, the physique intimidates and the speed surprises, he will invariably have a pose for each action, that is ... hits in a certain way, stops in a certain way way, eat in a certain way, are the kind of hobbies that all people we have, only on a heroic level.

It is rare that he only uses his hands, he usually has a weapon that works also defense, if you fall in love with a woman, or get married with her she either goes abroad or they kill her because a hero cannot maintain a normal relationship given his quality of savior.

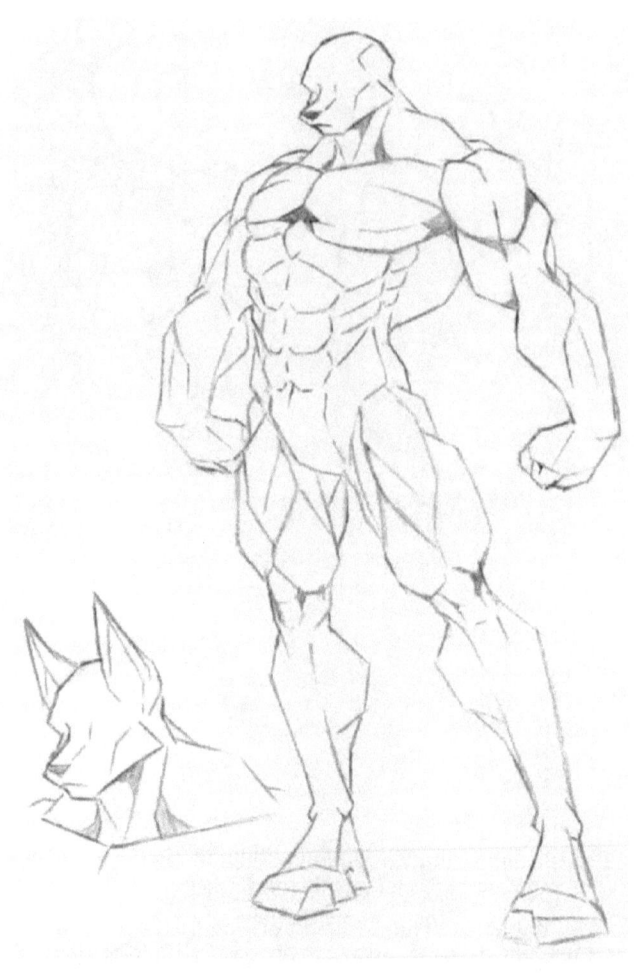

Think of all the exalted values of any human being,
Combine them with a little psychology and you will have your hero.
A hero who harms people for trying to do good
He is an Anti Hero who is like the Hero, but more Extreme ...
(What a contradiction, no?).

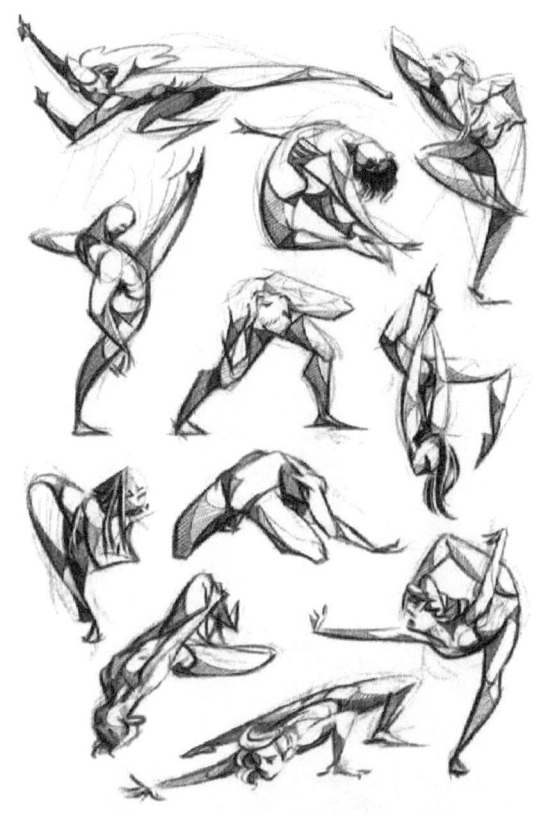

The second most important part of the super hero comic is ...
The Villain.

One cannot exist without the other, they are complementary opposites,
yin and yang, day and night, need each other to be able
bring the story.

The villain is Machiavellian, very intelligent, evil, his soul tortured
demands satisfaction by some means, be it violence, desire
of wealth or power, or the simple fact of seeing the faces of pain
in people.

47

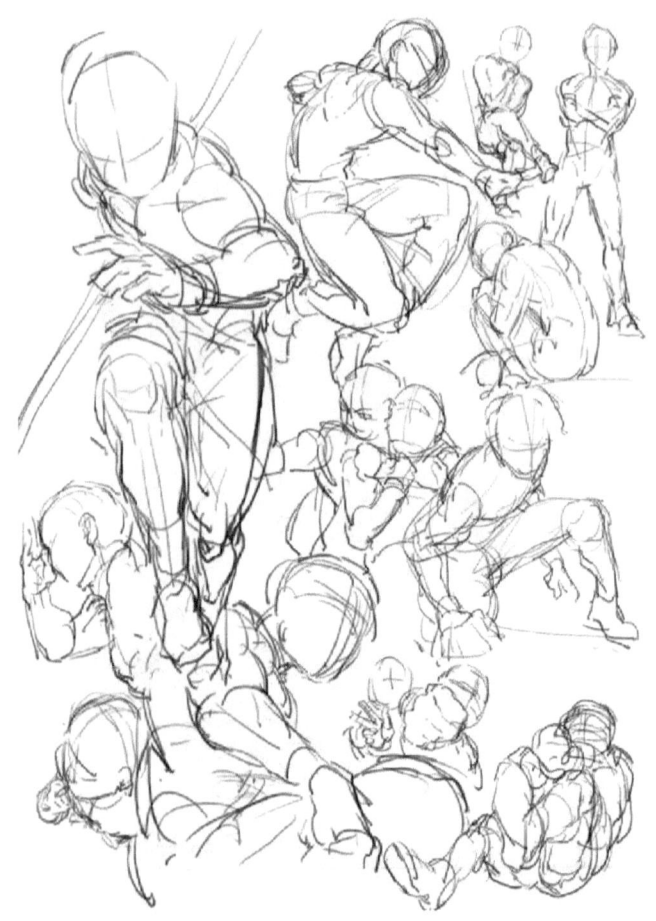

Like gender, they do not have a certain age, although as the
The villain's main characteristic is intelligence.
almost always older, old age is wisdom; However, there are thousands
of excuses for the villain to be a child.

Although military uniforms (symbol of conviction and discipline
with which they carry out their plans) are typically used,
a villain can truly wear any type of clothing.

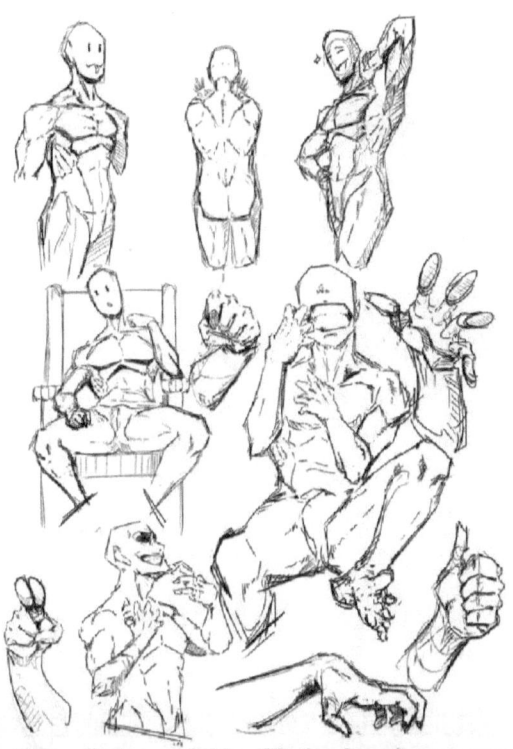

The poses of the villains, outside of being heroic, are many times lowered, craving when attacking and tired when standing, given that the hero always ruins his plans. When they win the pose is triumphant.

It is important that you develop the characteristics of your characters before drawing them and that you have very Present what kind of people they are, since the character It can get out of hand in your story without you realizing it.

Study in all these examples the differences between dynamism of villains and heroes.

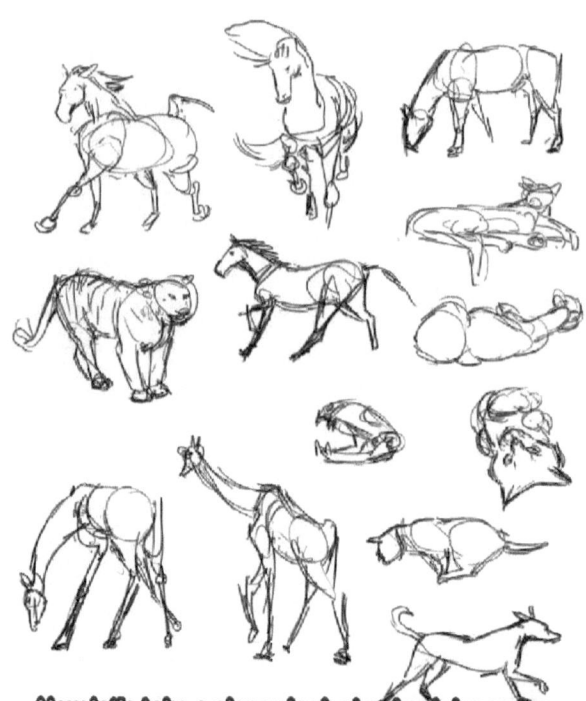

Now let's take a closer look at animal dynamics.

As you will see, the handling of the dynamic line in animals is not far a lot of how it is handled in humans. Spinal column follows the movement of the dynamic line and the rest of the structure docks with it.

You can also give your animals personality depending the type of line you choose, although they are more characteristic the final features.

Note: When drawing animals they always have a dynamic line curve, you should never use straight lines because that reduces their impact.

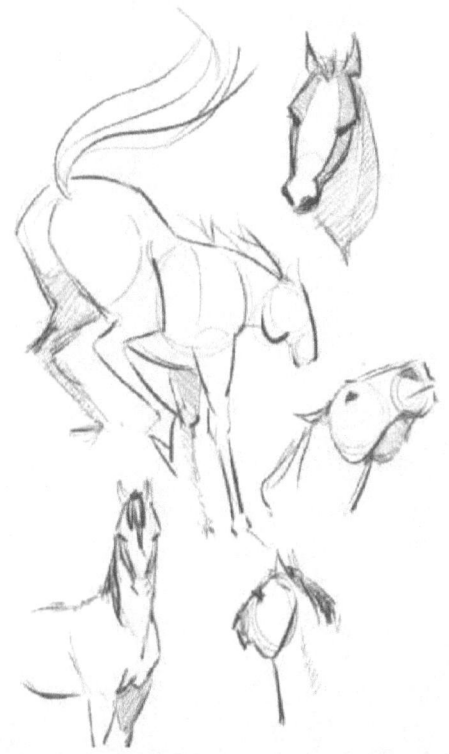

Finally when you want to mix animal and human.

The immense disproportion on the structure that makes
make our character look awesome.

Compare the size of the hands, with that of the head, the proportion
of the chest with respect to the legs, everything should be designed so that
our drawing looks impressive, they even get to sacrifice
some important laws like ankle width or other parts
of the normal body (although they would normally break with the weight,
or with the use in activities) but the priority is that the character
look and feel great.

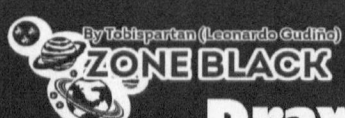

By Tobispartan (Leonardo Gudiño)
ZONE BLACK
Drawing Manual

Line
Dynamic

More from the Author

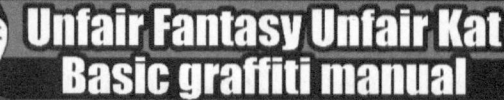

The Tao Of Drawing
Manual of he drew put Attitude
The great Newfoundland

Unfair Fantasy Unfair Kat
Basic graffiti manual

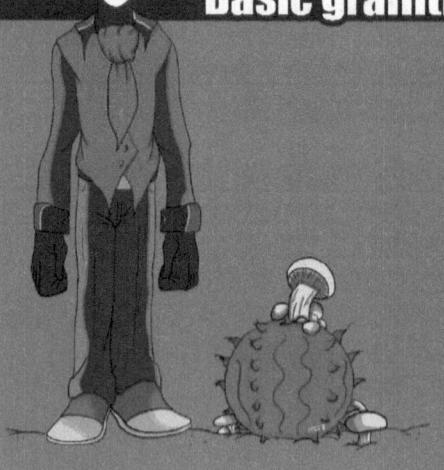

www.ingramcontent.com/pod-product-compliance
Lightning Source LLC
Chambersburg PA
CBHW030532220526
45463CB00007B/2799